Unsolved Mysteries

Phil Preece

Series Editors: Steve Barlow and Steve Skidmore

Published by Ginn and Company
Halley Court, Jordan Hill, Oxford OX2 8EJ
A division of Reed Educational and Professional Publishing Ltd
Telephone number for ordering **Impact**: 01865 888084

OXFORD MELBOURNE AUCKLAND JOHANNESBURG BLANTYRE
GABORONE IBADAN PORTSMOUTH (NH) USA CHICAGO

First published 1999

2003 2002 2001 2000 99

10 9 8 7 6 5 4 3 2 1

ISBN 0 435 21261 3

Illustrations
Chris Brown

Picture research
Helen Reilly

Cover artwork
Chris Swee / The Organisation

Designed by Shireen Nathoo Design

Printed and bound in Spain by Eldelvives

Acknowledgements
The Author and Publishers wish to thank the following for permission to reproduce
photographs on the pages noted:
The Mariners' Museum pp.4b, 20-21; Fortean pp.4c, 24, 27, Illustrated London News
Picture Library pp.5a, 19, 31; Ancient Art and Architecture Collection Ltd pp.5c, 34-5,
38-9, 43; NASA/Science Photo Library pp.5b, 44; Mary Evans Picture Library pp.6,
10-11, 40-41; *Fate Magazine* cover Llewellyn Publications/Fortean pp.12; Robert
Harding p.13; Corbis p.17; Topham pp.22-3; Don Douglas/Fortean p.29; Royal Air
Force/Royal Geographical Society p.36; Robert Scagell/Galaxy p.37.

Contents

Introduction

The universe is stranger than we can imagine. Many
mysteries have never been explained. Ships have become
invisible or mysteriously disappeared. Their crews have
vanished without trace. Fish have fallen from the sky.

Some people can walk on red-hot coals without pain or burning. Others can float on air.

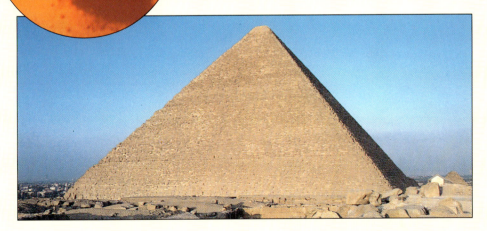

Some people have puzzled for centuries about the secrets of the pyramids in Egypt. Others believe a face can be seen on Mars. They wonder if this is proof of life in space.

Take a step into the unexpected. Welcome to the unsolved mysteries of the world.

The *Mary Celeste*

The strange story of the *Mary Celeste* is
the greatest shipping mystery of all time.
It has never been solved to this day.

The Mary Celeste

ABANDONED SHIP!

The *Mary Celeste* was an American sailing ship. It set out to cross the Atlantic in November 1872, taking goods to Italy. Benjamin Briggs was the captain. His family and the ship's crew were on board.

Three weeks later, a British ship found the *Mary Celeste*. It was sailing 650 kilometres from land with no one on board. No one from the *Mary Celeste* was ever seen or heard of again.

Evidence on board

A few clues were found on the ship.

- Stains looking like blood were found on the deck and the captain's sword.
- Two grooves were scratched into the ship's sides and the ship's rail was damaged.
- There were signs that the ship had been left in a hurry.
- One of the ship's lifeboats had been launched.
- Some important sailing equipment and files were missing.
- Fresh water, food and clothes were still on board.

SEA MONSTERS, MURDER OR POISON?

There are many theories about what might have happened to the *Mary Celeste*.

Theory 1: A sea monster

The crew may have been snatched by a giant octopus or squid from the depths of the sea. A giant squid was blamed for sinking another ship earlier in the 19th century. But the whole crew would have to have been on deck at the same time for this to happen.

Theory 2: Mutiny and murder

The crew may have got drunk on the **raw alcohol** the ship was taking to Italy. Then they could have murdered the captain and his family and escaped in the lifeboat. But raw alcohol is poisonous. The crew would have felt too ill to carry out their plan.

Theory 3: Poisoned food

The food and water on the *Mary Celeste* may have gone bad. Food poisoning could have made the crew **hallucinate**. As a result, they may have gone mad and jumped overboard. But when the *Mary Celeste* was found, the food and water were in good condition.

A STORM OR A FRAUD?

Theory 4: Stormy weather

A **waterspout** or **tornado** may have struck the ship. The crew may have thought they were about to sink and abandoned ship in a hurry. But the *Mary Celeste* showed no signs of damage from a waterspout or tornado when it was found.

Theory 5: Fraud

The main suspects are the crew of the British ship that found the *Mary Celeste*. The law of the sea says that people who find an abandoned ship can claim its value. The captains of both ships were friends. They could have plotted to share the money. Then they may have argued. As a result the whole crew could have been murdered. But no evidence for this has been found.

So what did happen to the *Mary Celeste*? We may never find out.

The lost land of Atlantis

DISASTER STRIKES!

In 400BCE, a Greek writer called **Plato** wrote about a 'lost land' called Atlantis. He heard about it from an Egyptian priest. Plato said that Atlantis was a huge and wealthy empire. He said that a great disaster suddenly struck the land. Violent earthquakes shook it. Great tidal waves covered it. Then Atlantis sank for ever beneath the sea.

Many people have tried to find the site of Atlantis, but it has not yet been discovered.

The people of Atlantis were said to be great builders. Their capital city was surrounded by beautiful canals. It had magnificent palaces and temples.

WHERE WAS ATLANTIS?

Theory 1: Land in sight?

Plato believed that Atlantis was in the Atlantic Ocean off the west coast of Africa. The Canary Islands are in this area. People have suggested that the Canary Islands are the mountain tops of Atlantis.

Are the Canary Islands the mountain tops of Atlantis?

Theory 2: Central America?

Some people have wondered if Atlantis was really part of Central America. The people there did have great cities long ago. They built huge pyramids before most other countries had built houses. But we now know those pyramids were built after Plato was told about Atlantis.

Theory 3: Explosion?

The Greek island of Santorini is the shell of a large dead volcano. It exploded about 3500 years ago in 1500BCE. It was one of the biggest eruptions in history. It caused earthquakes and huge tidal waves. The island was totally destroyed. Everyone on it died. Nearby, the great empire of Crete was also badly hit.

Plato wrote about Atlantis 1000 years after this explosion. Some people think that the story of Atlantis is really about the explosion on Santorini.

So was Atlantis a legend or was it a real place? If it was real, where was it? The search continues.

The Bermuda Triangle

MISSING!

The Bermuda Triangle is an area of the Atlantic Ocean. Travelling in this area can be a dangerous business! Many ships and planes have disappeared there without trace.

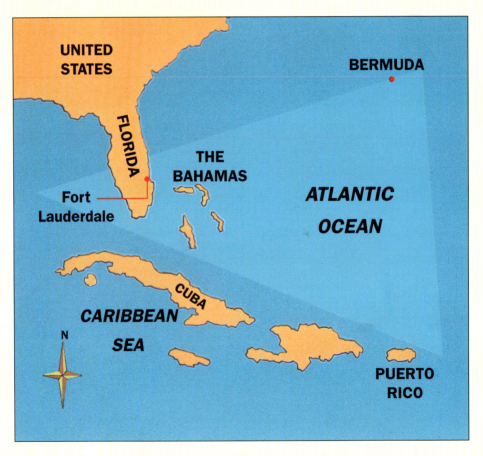

The Bermuda Triangle

Flight 19 never returned to base.

The story of the Bermuda Triangle began with a mysterious event in December 1945. A group of five American Avenger **torpedo** bombers went on a training flight. They took off from Fort Lauderdale, a naval air station in Florida. They flew across the Atlantic and over the islands of the Bahamas. The weather was clear and the flying conditions good.

But the bombers never returned. Their leader contacted base. He said the planes' compasses had stopped working. The bombers were lost. None of the planes or their crew was ever seen again.

WHAT HAPPENED?

People started to notice a pattern of disappearances in the Bermuda Triangle. At least another sixteen planes went missing soon after, as well as many ships. Many of the missing craft were first able to report that their instruments had failed. There are several theories about why ships and planes might vanish in this area.

Theory 1: Alien abductions

Some people believe the Triangle is the site of alien **abductions**. They say that UFOs might have been responsible for the disappearance of ships, planes and their crews. Perhaps aliens took them so they could study human beings.

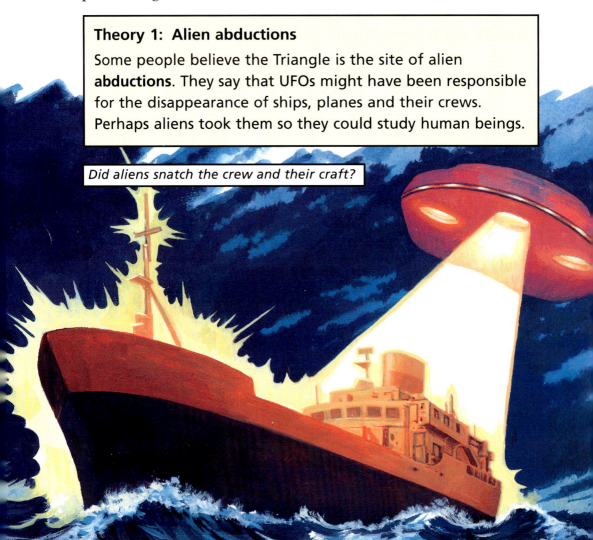

Did aliens snatch the crew and their craft?

Theory 2: Magnetic fields

There might be something wrong with the earth's **magnetic field** in this area. Instruments could stop working. With no direction-finding equipment, ships and planes lose their way.

Theory 3: Wild weather

The Bermuda Triangle covers thousands of square kilometres of the Atlantic Ocean. It is famous for having violent storms, including **hurricanes**. These can blow up very suddenly. Yet none of the missing ships and planes reported bad weather before they vanished.

All that was left of the S.S. Marine Sulphur Queen. *It vanished in the Triangle in 1963 with all her crew. What happened is still a mystery.*

The Philadelphia Experiment

Can a huge battleship with all its crew vanish and then reappear? This is what some people claim. They say it was a top-secret experiment carried out by the US Navy during the Second World War. It has come to be known as The Philadelphia Experiment.

DISAPPEARED!

In 1943, a sailor stood on the deck of his ship in Newport, Virginia. He was watching a ship called the *USS Eldridge*. It was a US Navy **destroyer**. As he looked, the air turned dark around the ship. A green mist seemed to cover it and spread outwards.

The USS Eldridge.

The next minute the sailor rubbed his eyes in disbelief. The ship had completely disappeared. All he could see was a slight dip in the sea where the ship's hull had been. Then, slowly, the *USS Eldridge* reappeared.

SECRETS AND LIES?

After the war, the sailor reported that he had seen the *USS Eldridge* disappear. He claimed that scientists had been testing a way to make ships invisible to the enemy's **radar**.

He said the US Government wanted to win the war quickly. So they risked experimenting on a ship with its crew on board.

But the experiment had a terrible effect on the crew. One newspaper reported that some of them died, while others went mad.

Since then, investigators have claimed that the ship did disappear.

The US Navy has always denied the story. Yet some people still think it may be true. Has the story been covered up because the experiment went wrong? Only when the US Navy releases its secret records might we know the truth.

Falling objects

For centuries there have been reports from all over the world about objects falling from the sky.

- Hundreds of live rats fell from the sky in Norway in 1680.
- A hail of pebbles and stones fell in England in 1973.
- A house in Lancashire was bombarded by falling apples in 1984.
- Other reports include falls of coins, lumps of coal, sweets, frogs, toads and fish.

A woodcut of fish falling from the skies, published in 1555.

In 1989, the Degen family were enjoying an ordinary day at their home in Queensland, Australia. Suddenly, thousands of sardines began to rain down on their house and garden. Where they came from was a mystery. Only the Degens' cat was happy about this strange rain – he had as many sardines as he could eat!

Is there an explanation?

People have often tried to explain the mystery of falling objects.

1   In ancient times, falling objects were often thought to be a gift from God.

2   French peasants reported seeing a great stone fall from the sky in 1768. Scientists at the time accused them of lying. People now think they saw a **meteor**.

3   Swarms of pink frogs fell during a rainstorm in Gloucestershire in England, in 1987. People believe they had been sucked up from the Sahara desert by freak winds.

Some falling objects can be explained. But what is the mystery behind the others?

Spontaneous human combustion

FIRE DEATH MYSTERY

Police officer John Heymer was called to investigate a mysterious house fire in Ebbw Vale, in Wales.

He opened the living room door carefully. At once he knew something was very wrong. In front of him on the floor was a pile of ash. From it stuck a pair of human feet, still wearing socks. A blackened skull lay nearby. Oily traces of burnt flesh coated the ceiling and light bulb. There were no other bodily remains.

The whole body of 73-year-old Henry Thomas had been destroyed by a fierce fire, apart from his feet. His leg bones were burnt to a white ash. Yet strangely his feet were completely unharmed. A settee nearby was not even scorched. Plastic tiles under the man's body had not melted, despite the heat.

Friday 6 January 1980

Some people believed Henry Thomas died from spontaneous human combustion. This is where people burst into flames without any warning. They seem to burn from the inside out.

People who have died from spontaneous human combustion are often elderly. Many have collapsed near to open fires. Their bodies seem to have burnt very quickly. Their bones have burnt to ash in the intense heat. Yet other parts of the body and objects nearby may be unharmed. No one has been able to explain what might cause these tragic deaths.

John Irving Bentley died mysteriously in America in 1966. Was this another case of spontaneous human combustion?

Mind over matter

FIREWALKING

Firewalking has taken place in different parts of the world for thousands of years. Firewalkers walk on burning coals or red-hot stones without getting burnt. The heat of the fire can be up to 800 degrees centigrade and the firewalkers' feet should be covered in blisters and burns. Yet they are not hurt at all.

One of the most amazing firewalks took place in India in 1921. It was staged for an Indian prince. The local holy man promised that the fire was safe. A frightened servant was pushed into the firepit to test it. But at once his fear turned to smiles as he was unharmed by the flames.

New fuel was heaped in the fiery pit. Then the prince's brass band marched into the flames. They all carried their musical instruments. Even their sheets of music were untouched by the flames that rose around them.

> It would seem impossible to walk on red-hot coals without getting hurt. No one should try it unless they have had expert preparation. But firewalking does happen. Some people say firewalkers may go into a kind of **trance** that stops them being hurt.

The coals are at their hottest, yet the firewalker has not been burnt.

LEVITATION

Some people seem to be able to float on air. This is known as **levitation**. People who levitate are often good at **yoga**. Do their minds have power to control their bodies?

Subbayah Pullavar was a yoga expert. A photograph was taken of him in 1936. He was levitating in front of a large crowd. He floated in the air in broad daylight for four minutes. His hand rested lightly on a stick. Witnesses checked but could find no other means of support. Then, very slowly, he sank back down to earth.

Subbayah Pullavar levitating in 1936.

Western science has investigated the power of yoga. But so far it has not succeeded in explaining how or why yoga and levitation work.

Out of Egypt

THE PYRAMIDS

There are more than 80 pyramids in Egypt. They were built to be royal tombs. The Great Pyramid is the largest. It is the biggest single building in the history of the world.

The Great Pyramid was built around 4500 years ago. It took about 20 years and around 100,000 men to build it. There is a maze of passages, shafts and hidden chambers inside the pyramid. No one knows what all of them were for.

People still do not know how the Egyptians had the skills to build such a great pyramid.

The Great Pyramid is near modern-day Cairo in Egypt.

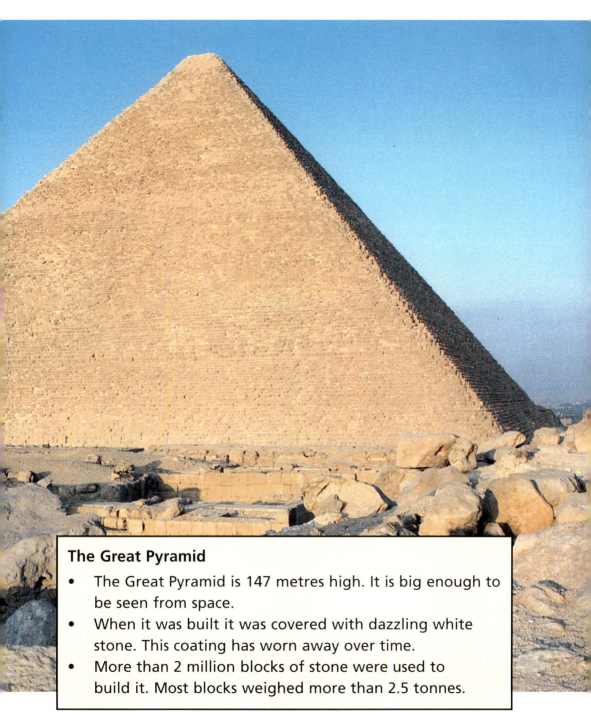

The Great Pyramid

- The Great Pyramid is 147 metres high. It is big enough to be seen from space.
- When it was built it was covered with dazzling white stone. This coating has worn away over time.
- More than 2 million blocks of stone were used to build it. Most blocks weighed more than 2.5 tonnes.

HOW WAS THE GREAT PYRAMID BUILT?

The ancient Egyptians who built the Great Pyramid had no modern equipment, such as wheels and pulleys, to help them.

Archaeologists have found wall paintings which show that they used ramps of earth to build some pyramids. The heavy blocks were hauled up the ramps on sledges. But to build a ramp big enough to make the Great Pyramid would have been almost impossible.

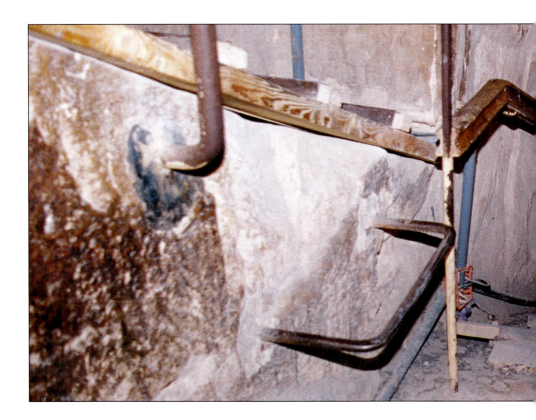

Where did the Egyptians learn their skills?

- No one really knows how the ancient Egyptians moved the millions of tonnes of rock to make the Great Pyramid.
- The stone was cut with great accuracy. Yet they only had chisels and hammers.
- The four sides of the Great Pyramid were built to face exactly north, east, south and west. The compass had not yet been invented, so how did the builders do it?

Inside the Great Pyramid. Many of the passages were built as traps to stop robbers getting in.

HIDDEN MEANINGS

Two other pyramids were built near the Great Pyramid at Giza. Some people claim the three pyramids make a ground map of the belt stars of the Orion star group.

Most Egyptians worshipped the sun. But one ancient King believed his **ancestor** was a god who came from the star group Orion.

Could there be a link between the pyramids and Orion? If so, the pyramids may hold an even deeper mystery that connects them with outer space.

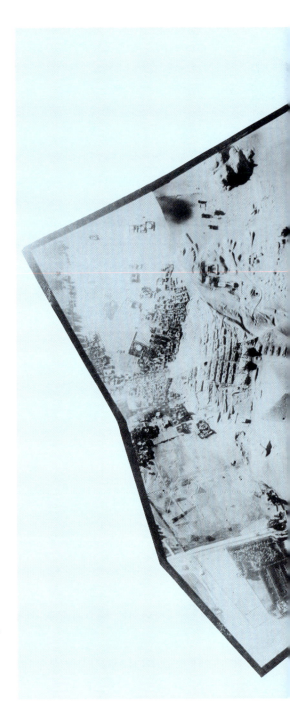

The Great Pyramid with two other pyramids at Giza. Could they be a ground map for the belt stars of the star group Orion?

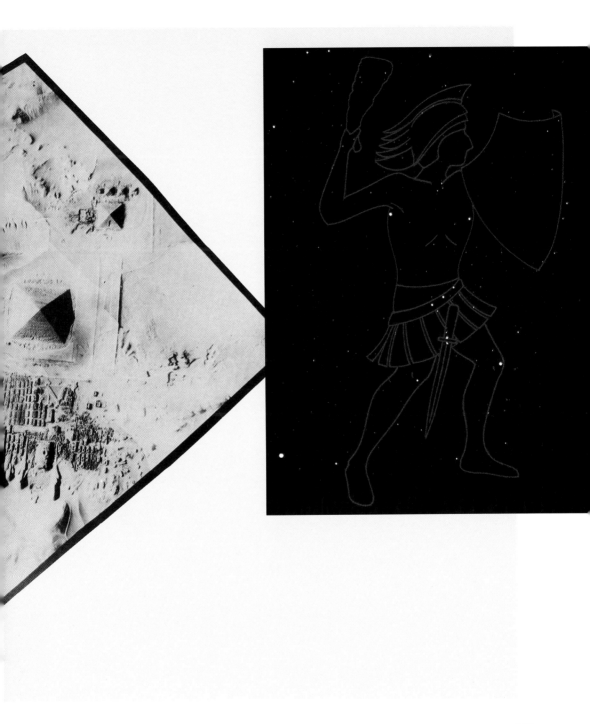

THE SPHINX

The Sphinx has stood in front of the pyramids for about 4500 years. It is 73 metres long and has the body of a lion and a human head. The head is a model of an Egyptian king called Khafre who died about 2500BCE.

Stories about sphinxes go back many years before the pyramids were built. They were huge creatures, both wise and dangerous.

However, no one knows what the Sphinx is for.

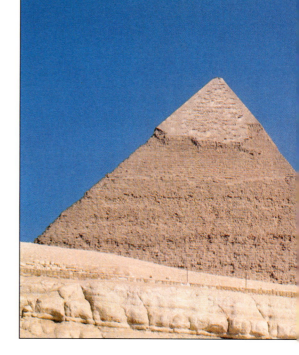

What secrets is the Sphinx guarding?

What is the secret of the Sphinx?

New electronic scans have shown there may be hidden chambers under the Sphinx. They might contain details about how the ancient Egyptians built the pyramids. Until the authorities allow anyone to dig there, the Sphinx will continue to guard its secret.

THE CURSE OF TUTANKHAMUN

On 26 November 1922, two archaeologists broke into a tomb in the Valley of the Kings, in Egypt. A boy-king called Tutankhamun had been buried there.

The archaeologists, Howard Carter and the Earl of Carnarvon, were the first people to see inside the tomb for over 3000 years.

It was said that a curse of death would be on anyone who disturbed Tutankhamun's body. Many people connected with the newly-opened tomb died mysteriously. Even today the curse may still be at work.

Howard Carter looking at Tutankhamun's coffin.

The archaeologists found priceless treasures in the tomb. There was a life-size figure of the king, a golden throne and beautiful jewellery. Tutankhamun was laid in a coffin made from solid gold.

SIGNS OF THE CURSE?

The first sign of the curse appeared when a cobra killed Howard Carter's pet canary. The ancient Egyptians believed cobras were royal snakes. Their task was to guard the king. The local people said it was a sign that another death would follow. They said Tutankhamun's tomb should never have been broken open.

Then the Earl of Carnarvon fell ill after being bitten by a mosquito. He died on 4 April 1923 in Cairo. At the moment of his death all the lights in Cairo suddenly went out. No one has ever been able to explain why.

Back in England, at the same moment, the Earl's dog began to howl and then died. The legend of the curse had begun.

Soon more deaths were linked to Tutankhamun's tomb.

- Three of Howard Carter's assistants died.
- Professor La Fleur was an archaeologist who had rushed to Egypt to see Tutankhamun's tomb. He died that very night.

Bad luck also seemed to follow the tomb's treasures.

- The treasures were taken to London for an exhibition in 1972. A newspaper reporter asked the person organising the exhibition if he believed in the curse. The organiser laughed at the idea. Four weeks later he was dead.

Tutankhamun's Mummy–restoration. ▶

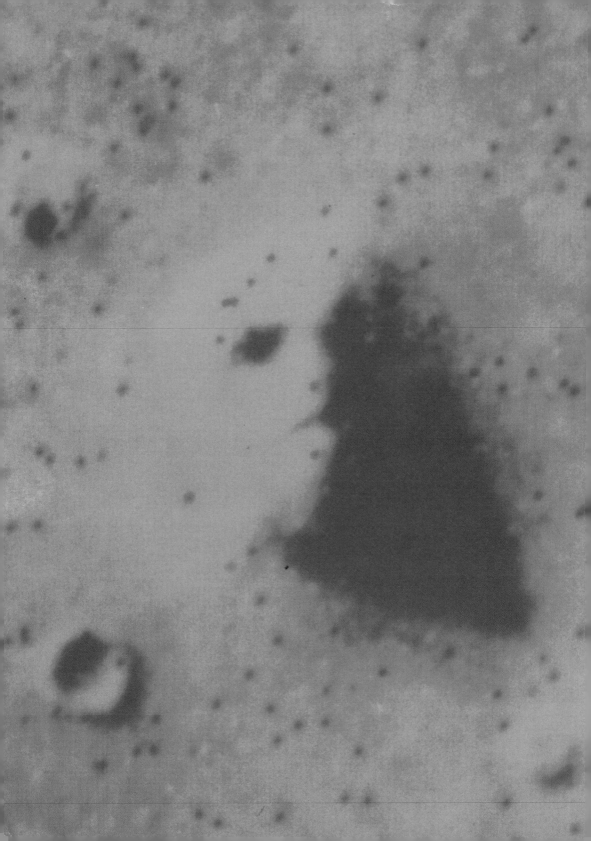

A face on Mars?

On 25 July 1976, the Viking 1 space probe was circling the planet Mars. It was taking photographs of possible landing spots. When the photographs were beamed back to earth, it was possible to see a mountain in the shape of a human head. It was 1.5 kilometres across. Some people say the face proves there was once life on Mars.

NASA says the photographs do not show anything unusual. They claim the head is no more than a rock. They say that shadows make it look as if it has eyes, a nose and a mouth. Some people believe NASA are covering up the truth. Have they really found proof of life elsewhere in space?

◄ *The face on Mars.*

WHAT OTHER MYSTERIES ARE OUT THERE?

There are still many questions we cannot answer. More mysteries may be waiting for us as we reach out to the stars. How many of them will ever be solved? The universe is stranger than we can possibly imagine.

Glossary

abduction To kidnap somebody. *page 18*

ancestor A person we are descended from. *page 36*

archaeologist (*arki-olla-jist*) Someone who studies the people and
    remains of ancient times. *page 34*

destroyer A type of fast warship used against submarines. *page 20*

hallucinate (*ha-loosi-nate*) To see strange images or visions. *page 9*

hurricane A type of violent tropical storm. *page 19*

levitation Floating weightlessly on air. *page 30*

magnetic field The pulling force with which a magnet attracts
    things. *page 19*

meteor A rock-like object that flies through space. *page 25*

Plato (*Play-toe*) A Greek thinker and writer who lived about
    427–347 BCE. *page 12*

radar   A way of finding objects by bouncing radio beams off
    them. Any solid object gives a radar trace. The radar trace
    shows where an object is, how big it is and how fast it is
    moving. *page 22*

raw alcohol A chemical used in industry. *page 9*

trance A state that is similar to sleep. *page 28*

tornado A type of whirlwind. *page 10*

torpedo An underwater weapon. *page 17*

waterspout A tornado or high wind that happens over water and forms a column of water. *page 10*

yoga An eastern system of exercises that helps people to control their minds and bodies. *page 30*

Index